GW00888632

contents

NZ, Canada, US and UK readers
Please note that Australian cup and spoon
measurements are metric. A quick conversion
guide appears on page 63.

risotto # know-how

Risotto, a creamy rice dish originally from northern Italy, is now so wildly popular it's almost impossible to find a cafe or restaurant menu on which it doesn't feature. So, what are the secrets to perfecting this comforting dish at home?

The beauty of learning how to make risotto is that, while every recipe loosely follows the same basic method, you can chop and change it to your liking – take shortcuts for a quick family meal, make a hearty main with meat, seafood or poultry, or even re-do the original concept, making the final product dry or soupy, soft or firm to the bite, subtle or highly spiced. The bottom line is that risotto is a moveable feast, happy to adjust to its maker's whim.

The right rice

Using the correct variety of rice is vital if you want to cook a memorable risotto. The rice must be a short, round grain; the most commonly available risotto rice is arborio, which can be purchased in most supermarkets. Arborio rice has a soft texture and chalky centre; during the cooking process, the rice grains release starch, giving the dish its creaminess.

Hot stock

The rice in a risotto is cooked, via the absorption method, in hot stock or other liquid. The important point to remember is that the cooking liquid must be already hot when it is added to the rice. Keep hot liquid in a separate saucepan, at a low simmer, as the risotto takes shape.

Patience is a virtue

Making risotto isn't a particularly lengthy process, but it does require your undivided attention and a little patience. A risotto needs to be stirred constantly and watched closely to ensure it doesn't stick to the base of the saucepan. On top of that, you should only add a small portion of the hot cooking liquid at a time; stir the risotto until each portion is completely absorbed before adding the next.

4 roasted capsicum risotto
with barbecued prawns

2 tablespoons olive oil

2 cloves garlic, crushed

2 cups (400g) arborio rice

1 cup (250ml) dry white wine

2½ cups (625ml) chicken stock

2 small red capsicums (300g)

½ cup (125ml) cream

1 cup (250ml) milk

1 tablespoon coarsely chopped fresh coriander leaves

barbecued prawns

500g medium uncooked prawns

1 tablespoon olive oil

1 teaspoon cracked black pepper

2 teaspoons lime juice

Heat oil in large saucepan; cook garlic until fragrant. Add rice, stir to coat in oil mixture. Add wine; cook over low heat, stirring, until liquid is absorbed. Add stock; bring to a boil. Reduce heat; simmer, covered, 15 minutes, stirring midway through cooking.

Meanwhile, quarter capsicums, remove and discard seeds and membranes. Roast under grill or in very hot oven, skin-side up, until skin blisters and blackens. Cover capsicum pieces with plastic or paper for 5 minutes, peel away skin. Blend or process capsicum with cream until almost smooth.

Stir capsicum puree and milk into risotto; cook, stirring, 5 minutes. Remove pan from heat; stand, covered, 5 minutes. Stir in coriander; serve with Barbecued Prawns.

Barbecued Prawns Shell and devein prawns, leaving tails intact. Toss prawns with remaining ingredients in medium bowl. Barbecue (or grill or char-grill) prawns until just changed in colour.

SERVES 4
Per serving 31.4g fat; 3244kJ

6 mushroom and

sun-dried tomato risotto

1 litre (4 cups) chicken stock

2 cups (500ml) water

1 cup (250ml) dry white wine

2 tablespoons olive oil

30g butter

200g button mushrooms, sliced thinly

200g flat mushrooms, sliced thinly

1 medium leek (350g), sliced thinly

2 cloves garlic, crushed

2 cups (400g) arborio rice

1/2 cup (40g) finely grated parmesan cheese

1/3 cup (50g) sun-dried tomatoes in oil, drained, sliced thinly

1 tablespoon finely chopped fresh oregano leaves

Bring stock, the water and wine to a boil in medium saucepan; reduce heat, cover, keep hot.
Heat oil and butter in large saucepan; cook mushrooms, leek and garlic, stirring, until leek is soft. Add rice, stir to coat in oil mixture. Stir in 1 cup of the stock mixture; cook over low heat, stirring, until liquid is absorbed.
Continue adding stock mixture in 1-cup batches, stirring, until absorbed after each addition. Total cooking time should be about
35 minutes or until rice is just tender. Remove pan from heat, stir in remaining ingredients.

SERVES 4
Per serving 24.1g fat; 2896kJ

buttery wine risotto with
smoked salmon

1.5 litres (6 cups) chicken stock

1 cup (250ml) dry white wine

40g butter

1 medium leek (350g), chopped finely

2 cloves garlic, crushed

2 cups (400g) arborio rice

$1/4$ teaspoon ground turmeric

40g butter, chopped finely, extra

$1/2$ cup (40g) finely grated parmesan cheese

100g smoked salmon, chopped coarsely

2 teaspoons finely chopped fresh dill

50g baby spinach leaves

Bring stock and wine to a boil in medium saucepan; reduce heat, cover, keep hot.

Heat butter in large saucepan; cook leek and garlic, stirring, until leek is very soft. Add rice and turmeric, stir to coat in butter mixture. Stir in 1 cup of the stock mixture; cook, stirring, over low heat until liquid is absorbed.

Continue adding stock mixture, in 1-cup batches, stirring after each addition. Total cooking time should be about 35 minutes or until rice is tender. Remove pan from heat, stir in extra butter, cheese, salmon, dill and spinach.

SERVES 4
Per serving 23.1g fat; 2824kJ

saffron lime risotto
with seafood

2 cups (500ml)
fish stock

1 litre (4 cups)
chicken stock

½ cup (125ml) dry
white wine

500g medium
uncooked prawns

20 medium black
mussels (500g)

¼ cup (60ml) olive oil

250g scallops

1 cup (250ml) water

2 cloves garlic, crushed

1 teaspoon grated
fresh ginger

½ teaspoon
saffron threads

2 cups (400g)
arborio rice

2 tablespoons
lime juice

½ teaspoon finely
grated lime rind

2 tablespoons coarsely
chopped fresh
coriander leaves

Bring both stocks and wine to a boil in medium saucepan; reduce heat, cover, keep hot. Shell and devein prawns, leaving tails intact. Scrub mussels, remove beards.

Heat 1 tablespoon of the oil in large saucepan; cook prawns and scallops until just changed in colour, remove from pan. Add the water to pan, bring to a boil. Add mussels; simmer, covered, until mussels open. Remove mussels from pan; discard liquid and any unopened mussels.

Heat remaining oil in same pan; cook garlic and ginger until fragrant; add saffron and rice, stir to coat in oil mixture. Stir in 1 cup of the stock mixture; cook, stirring, over low heat until liquid is absorbed.

Continue adding stock mixture, in 1-cup batches, stirring, until absorbed after each addition. Total cooking time should be about 35 minutes or until rice is just tender. Remove pan from heat; stir in seafood, juice, rind and coriander.

SERVES 4
Per serving 16.7g fat; 2704kJ

asparagus
risotto

500g asparagus, chopped coarsely

3½ cups (875ml) chicken stock

3½ cups (875ml) water

30g butter

1 tablespoon olive oil

1 large brown onion (200g), chopped finely

3 bacon rashers, chopped finely

1 clove garlic, crushed

2 cups (400g) arborio rice

¾ cup (60g) finely grated parmesan cheese

2 tablespoons finely chopped fresh flat-leaf parsley

Boil, steam or microwave asparagus until just tender; drain, rinse under cold water, drain.
Bring stock and the water to a boil in medium saucepan; reduce heat, cover, keep hot. Heat butter and oil in large saucepan; cook onion, bacon and garlic, stirring, until onion is soft. Add rice, stir to coat in oil mixture. Stir in 1 cup of the stock mixture; cook over low heat, stirring, until liquid is absorbed.
Continue adding stock mixture, in 1-cup batches, stirring, until absorbed after each addition. Total cooking time should be 35 minutes or until rice is tender. Stir in asparagus, cheese and parsley.

SERVES 4
Per serving 19.5g fat; 2562kJ

mixed mushroom and
cheese risotto

*10g dried porcini
mushrooms*

1 cup (250ml) boiling water

*1 litre (4 cups)
chicken stock*

1½ cups (375ml) water

40g butter

2 tablespoons olive oil

*2 medium brown onions
(300g), chopped finely*

*200g cup mushrooms,
sliced thinly*

2 cups (400g) arborio rice

*1 cup (80g) finely grated
parmesan cheese*

Place porcini mushrooms in medium heatproof bowl, cover with
the boiling water, stand 30 minutes. Drain mushrooms, reserve
½ cup (125ml) of liquid.

Bring reserved liquid from mushrooms, stock and the water to
a boil in medium saucepan; reduce heat, cover, keep hot.

Heat butter and oil in large saucepan; cook onion and all the mushrooms,
stirring, until onion is soft. Add rice, stir to coat in oil mixture. Stir in 1 cup
of the stock mixture; cook over low heat, stirring, until liquid is absorbed.

Continue adding stock mixture, in 1-cup batches, stirring, until absorbed
after each addition. Total cooking time should be about 35 minutes or until
rice is just tender. Stir in cheese.

SERVES 4
Per serving 25.6g fat; 2764kJ

12 risotto cakes

1 tablespoon olive oil

1 medium brown onion
(150g), chopped finely

1 clove garlic, crushed

3 cups (600g)
calrose rice

1 cup (250ml) dry
white wine

3 cups (750ml)
chicken stock

2 cups (500ml) water

1 cup (125g) frozen
peas, thawed

1/3 cup (50g) plain flour

vegetable oil, for
shallow-frying

6 bacon rashers

basil cream

2 teaspoons olive oil

1 small brown onion
(80g), chopped finely

1 clove garlic, crushed

1/4 cup (60ml) dry
white wine

300ml cream

1/3 cup coarsely
chopped fresh
basil leaves

with crisp bacon and basil cream

Heat olive oil in large saucepan; cook onion and garlic, stirring, until onion is soft. Add rice, stir to coat in oil mixture. Add wine; cook over low heat, stirring, until liquid is absorbed. Add stock and the water; bring to a boil. Reduce heat; simmer, uncovered, stirring occasionally, until rice is just tender and liquid absorbed. Gently stir in peas; cool 30 minutes.

Shape 1/2-cups of rice mixture into patties; place on tray. Coat patties in flour, shake off excess. Heat vegetable oil in large frying pan; shallow-fry patties, in batches, until browned both sides and heated through. Drain risotto cakes on absorbent paper. Drain oil from pan; cook bacon until browned and crisp. Drain on absorbent paper. Serve risotto cakes with bacon and Basil Cream.

Basil Cream Heat oil in small saucepan; cook onion and garlic, stirring, until onion is soft. Add wine; cook, stirring, about 3 minutes or until liquid has evaporated. Stir in cream, bring to a boil; simmer, uncovered, about 10 minutes or until sauce thickens slightly. Stir in basil; simmer, uncovered, 5 minutes. Strain sauce over small bowl; discard onion mixture. Return sauce to same pan; simmer, stirring, until hot.

SERVES 6
Per serving 30.9g fat; 3175kJ

risotto marinara

2 tablespoons olive oil

1 medium brown onion (150g), chopped finely

2 cups (400g) arborio rice

3$\frac{1}{2}$ cups (875ml) hot vegetable stock

750g medium uncooked prawns, shelled

500g seafood marinara mix

$\frac{1}{2}$ cup (125ml) cream

$\frac{1}{2}$ cup (40g) coarsely grated parmesan cheese

Heat oil in large saucepan; cook onion, stirring, until soft. Add rice; stir to coat in oil mixture. Add hot stock; simmer, covered, about 15 minutes, or until liquid is absorbed, stirring midway through cooking.
Meanwhile, cut prawns in half through their backs, combine with marinara mix. Stir seafood into risotto; simmer, covered, about 7 minutes or until seafood has changed in colour.
Remove pan from heat, stir in cream and cheese; stand, covered, 2 minutes.

SERVES 4
Per serving 31.6g fat; 3698kJ

roasted risotto-filled
capsicums

4 large red capsicums (1.4kg)

1 cup (70g) stale breadcrumbs

1 cup (80g) finely grated parmesan cheese

1 tablespoon olive oil

risotto

1 tablespoon olive oil

200g minced lamb

1 medium brown onion (150g), chopped finely

1 clove garlic, crushed

1/2 teaspoon ground cinnamon

1/2 cup (100g) calrose rice

400g can tomatoes

1 cup (250ml) chicken stock

Halve capsicums lengthways, discard seeds and membranes. Place capsicum on large oven tray; bake, uncovered, in hot oven 15 minutes. Using absorbent paper, pat dry the inside of capsicum halves.

Spoon in hot Risotto; top with combined crumbs and cheese; drizzle with oil. Bake, uncovered, in hot oven about 15 minutes or until capsicums are soft and topping is browned.

Risotto Heat oil in medium saucepan; cook lamb, stirring, until browned. Add onion, garlic and cinnamon; cook, stirring, until onion is soft. Add rice, stir to coat in oil mixture. Add undrained crushed tomatoes and stock, bring to a boil; reduce heat, simmer, covered, 15 minutes, stirring midway through cooking. Remove from heat; stand, covered, 10 minutes.

SERVES 4
Per serving 21.2g fat; 2115kJ

marinated lamb,
rosemary and garlic risotto

500g lamb fillets

3 cloves garlic, crushed

1 tablespoon olive oil

1 tablespoon balsamic vinegar

1.5 litres (6 cups) beef stock

1 cup (250ml) dry white wine

2 tablespoons olive oil, extra

1 medium brown onion (150g), sliced thinly

1 clove garlic, crushed, extra

2 cups (400g) arborio rice

1/2 cup (100g) char-grilled capsicum in oil, drained, sliced thinly

2 tablespoons fresh rosemary

Combine lamb, garlic, oil and vinegar in medium bowl; cover, stand 10 minutes.

Bring stock and wine to a boil in medium saucepan; reduce heat, cover, keep hot.

Heat extra oil in large saucepan; cook onion, stirring, until browned lightly. Add garlic; cook until fragrant. Add rice, stir to coat in oil mixture. Stir in 1 cup of the stock mixture; cook over low heat, stirring, until liquid is absorbed.

Continue adding stock mixture, in 1-cup batches, stirring, until absorbed after each addition. Total cooking time should be about 35 minutes or until rice is just tender.

Meanwhile, cook lamb, in batches, on heated oiled grill plate (or grill or barbecue) until browned all over and cooked as desired. Slice lamb thickly.

Remove risotto from heat, stir in lamb, capsicum and rosemary.

SERVES 4
Per serving 26.7g fat; 3407kJ

fish risotto

1 tablespoon
vegetable oil

1 medium brown onion
(150g), sliced thinly

1 medium red
capsicum (200g),
sliced thinly

1 teaspoon
curry powder

1 cup (200g)
calrose rice

2 cups (500ml) water

2 medium tomatoes
(380g), peeled,
chopped finely

500g boneless
white fish fillets,
chopped coarsely

2 tablespoons finely
chopped fresh
flat-leaf parsley

Heat oil in large saucepan; cook onion and
capsicum, stirring, until onion is soft. Add curry
powder and rice, stir to coat in oil mixture.
Stir in the water and tomato; bring to a boil.
Reduce heat; simmer, covered, stirring
occasionally, about 10 minutes or until
most of the liquid has been absorbed.
Stir in fish; simmer, covered, about 10 minutes
or until fish is just changed in colour and rice
is tender. Serve sprinkled with parsley.

SERVES 4
Per serving 7.9g fat; 1593kJ

cheesy salami and olive risotto

2 tablespoons olive oil

2 medium brown onions (300g), chopped finely

1 clove garlic, crushed

2 cups (400g) arborio rice

400g can tomatoes

3 cups (750ml) chicken stock

100g sliced mild salami, chopped coarsely

$1/2$ cup (75g) sun-dried tomatoes in oil, drained, sliced thickly

1 cup (160g) seeded black olives

$2/3$ cup (50g) coarsely grated parmesan cheese

$1/4$ teaspoon cracked black pepper

1 tablespoon finely shredded fresh sage leaves

Heat oil in large saucepan; cook onion and garlic, stirring, until onion is soft. Add rice, stir to coat in oil mixture. Add undrained crushed canned tomatoes and stock. Bring to a boil; reduce heat, simmer, covered, 15 minutes, stirring midway through cooking. Remove pan from heat; stand, covered, 10 minutes. Stir in remaining ingredients.

SERVES 4

Per serving 29.8g fat; 3218kJ

fresh salmon and sun-dried tomato risotto

1.5 litres (6 cups)
chicken stock

1 cup (250ml) dry
white wine

2 (400g) Atlantic
salmon fillets

¼ cup (60ml) olive oil

1 medium leek (350g),
sliced thinly

1 clove garlic, crushed

2 cups (400g)
arborio rice

½ cup (125ml) cream

¾ cup (110g) sun-
dried tomatoes
in oil, drained,
chopped coarsely

50g baby spinach
leaves, chopped
coarsely

2 tablespoons
finely shredded
fresh basil leaves

1 teaspoon cracked
black pepper

Bring stock and wine to a boil in medium saucepan; reduce heat, cover, keep hot.

Remove skin and bones from salmon. Heat 1 tablespoon of the oil in large non-stick frying pan; cook salmon both sides, uncovered, until just tender. Remove from pan; flake salmon with fork.

Heat remaining oil in large saucepan; cook leek and garlic, stirring, until leek is soft. Add rice, stir to coat in oil mixture. Stir in 1 cup of the stock mixture; cook over low heat, stirring, until liquid is absorbed.

Continue adding stock mixture, in 1-cup batches, stirring, until absorbed after each addition. Total cooking time should be about 35 minutes or until rice is just tender.

Add cream and tomatoes; cook, stirring, until risotto is thick and creamy. Remove pan from heat, gently stir in salmon, spinach, basil and pepper.

SERVES 4
Per serving 44.5g fat; 4006kJ

peperoni risotto

150g green
beans, halved

1.75 litres (7 cups)
chicken stock

2 tablespoons
tomato paste

1 tablespoon olive oil

20g butter

1 large brown onion
(200g), chopped finely

1 medium red
capsicum (200g),
chopped finely

2 cups (400g)
arborio rice

200g peperoni,
sliced thinly

1/3 cup (50g) pimiento-
stuffed green olives

Boil, steam or microwave beans until just tender, rinse under cold water; drain. Bring stock and paste to a boil in medium saucepan; reduce heat, cover, keep hot. Heat oil and butter in large saucepan; cook onion and capsicum, stirring, until onion is soft. Add rice, stir to coat in oil mixture. Stir in 1 cup of the stock mixture; cook, stirring, over low heat until liquid is absorbed. **Continue** adding stock mixture, in 1-cup batches, stirring, until absorbed after each addition. Total cooking time should be about 35 minutes or until rice is just tender. Remove pan from heat, stir in beans, peperoni and olives.

SERVES 4
Per serving 31g fat; 3092kJ

baked risotto with
spinach and salmon

2 tablespoons olive oil

1 medium brown onion
(150g), chopped finely

1 cup (200g) calrose rice

3 cups (750ml)
chicken stock

1/2 cup (125ml) cream

1 cup (125g) coarsely
grated cheddar cheese

1 cup (80g) finely grated
parmesan cheese

75g baby spinach leaves

415g can red
salmon, drained

pinch sweet paprika

Heat oil in medium saucepan; cook onion, stirring, until soft. Add rice, stir to coat in oil mixture. Add stock; bring to a boil. Reduce heat; simmer, covered, 15 minutes, stirring midway through cooking. Remove pan from heat; stand, covered, 10 minutes. Stir in cream and half of the combined cheeses.
Spoon half of the hot risotto into shallow 2-litre (8-cup) oiled ovenproof dish. Top with spinach and flaked salmon; spoon over remaining risotto. Sprinkle with remaining combined cheeses, then paprika.
Bake, uncovered, in very hot oven about 10 minutes or until browned lightly and heated through.

SERVES 4
Per serving 47.8g fat; 3155kJ

risotto with baked ricotta,
roasted onion
and tomatoes

1.5 litres (6 cups)
chicken stock

1 cup (250ml) dry
white wine

2 tablespoons olive oil

1 medium brown onion
(150g), chopped finely

2 cups (400g) arborio rice

1/4 cup (60ml) cream

1 tablespoon coarsely
chopped fresh sage leaves

1/4 cup (20g) finely grated
romano cheese

200g piece baked ricotta,
sliced thickly

1/2 cup (80g) seeded
black olives

**roasted onion and
tomatoes**

2 tablespoons olive oil

1 tablespoon brown sugar

1 tablespoon
balsamic vinegar

8 baby brown onions
(200g), halved

250g cherry
tomatoes, halved

Bring stock and wine to a boil in medium
saucepan; reduce heat, cover, keep hot.
Heat oil in large saucepan; cook onion,
stirring, until soft. Add rice, stir to coat
in oil mixture. Stir in 1 cup of the stock
mixture; cook over low heat, stirring, until
liquid is absorbed.
Continue adding stock mixture, in 1-cup
batches, stirring, until absorbed after each
addition. Total cooking time should be
about 35 minutes or until rice is just tender.
Remove pan from heat, gently stir in
cream, sage, cheese, baked ricotta, olives
and Roasted Onion and Tomatoes.
Roasted Onions and Tomatoes Combine
oil, sugar, vinegar and onions in medium
bowl. Transfer mixture to medium non-stick
baking dish; bake, uncovered, in very
hot oven about 10 minutes or until onions
are browned and just tender. Remove
dish from oven, add tomatoes; toss gently
until heated through.

SERVES 4
Per serving 34.1g fat; 3420kJ

kumara and
fennel risotto

1.5 litres (6 cups) chicken stock

2 tablespoons olive oil

1 medium brown onion (150g), chopped finely

1 clove garlic, crushed

1¹/₃ cups (265g) arborio rice

pinch saffron powder

¹/₂ small fennel bulb (150g), sliced thinly

150g kumara, sliced thickly

¹/₃ cup (25g) finely grated parmesan cheese

¹/₄ cup finely chopped fresh chives

Bring stock to a boil in medium saucepan; reduce heat, cover, keep hot. Heat oil in large saucepan; cook onion and garlic, stirring, until onion is soft. Add rice, saffron and fennel, stir to coat in oil mixture. Stir in 1 cup of the stock; cook, stirring, over low heat until liquid is absorbed. **Continue** adding stock in 1-cup batches, stirring, until absorbed after each addition. When about half of the stock has been added, add kumara; cook, stirring, while adding remaining stock in stages. Total cooking time should be about 35 minutes or until rice is just tender. **Serve** topped with cheese and chives.

SERVES 4
Per serving 13.1g fat; 1766kJ

vegetable risotto

1 litre (4 cups) vegetable stock

400g can tomatoes

1 tablespoon olive oil

1 medium leek (350g),
sliced thinly

2 cloves garlic, crushed

1½ cups (300g) arborio rice

1 small red capsicum (150g),
chopped finely

2 small yellow zucchini
(180g), sliced thinly

2 baby eggplants (120g),
sliced thinly

100g baby spinach leaves

½ cup (80g) seeded
black olives

¼ cup (20g) finely grated
parmesan cheese

Bring stock and undrained crushed tomatoes to a boil in medium
saucepan; reduce heat, cover, keep hot. Heat oil in large saucepan;
cook leek and garlic, stirring, until leek is soft. Add rice and capsicum, stir
to coat in oil mixture. Stir in 1 cup of the stock mixture; cook, stirring,
over low heat until liquid is absorbed.

Continue adding stock mixture, in 1-cup batches, stirring, until absorbed
after each addition. When about half of the stock has been added, add
zucchini and eggplant; cook, stirring, while adding remaining stock in
stages. Total cooking time should be about 35 minutes or until rice is
just tender. Remove pan from heat, add spinach, olives and cheese.

SERVES 4
Per serving 8.5g fat; 1785kJ

gremolata fish on
pumpkin risotto

750g piece
pumpkin

2 tablespoons
vegetable oil

2 teaspoons
garam masala

2 tablespoons
olive oil

1 small brown
onion (80g),
sliced thinly

1 clove garlic,
crushed

2 cups (400g)
calrose rice

1 litre (4 cups)
chicken stock

100g baby
spinach leaves

gremolata fish

1/3 cup finely
chopped fresh
flat-leaf parsley

1 tablespoon
vegetable oil

1 teaspoon finely
grated lemon rind

2 cloves garlic,
crushed

4 small (600g)
white fish fillets

Peel pumpkin, cut into 3cm pieces. Combine pumpkin, vegetable oil and garam masala in large non-stick baking dish. Bake, uncovered, in very hot oven about 15 minutes or until pumpkin is browned and just tender.
Meanwhile, heat olive oil in large saucepan; cook onion and garlic, stirring, until onion is soft. Add rice, stir to coat in oil mixture. Add stock; bring to a boil. Reduce heat; simmer, covered, 15 minutes, stirring midway through cooking. Remove pan from heat; stand, covered, 10 minutes.
Gently stir in pumpkin and spinach; stand, covered, 2 minutes. Serve topped with Gremolata Fish.
Gremolata Fish Combine parsley, oil, rind and garlic in medium bowl; press onto fish fillets. Cook fish in heated oiled large non-stick frying pan until browned both sides and just cooked through.

SERVES 4
Per serving 28.8g fat; 3434kJ

prawn and
asparagus risotto

32 medium
uncooked prawns
(approximately 1kg)

500g fresh asparagus

1.5 litres (6 cups)
chicken stock

1 1/2 cups (375ml)
dry white wine

30g butter

1 large brown onion
(200g), chopped finely

2 cloves garlic,
crushed

3 cups (600g)
arborio rice

2 medium tomatoes
(380g), seeded,
chopped finely

1/3 cup loosely packed,
coarsely chopped
fresh flat-leaf parsley

1/2 teaspoon cracked
black pepper

Shell and devein prawns, leaving tails intact. Slice asparagus diagonally into 3cm lengths.

Combine stock and wine in large saucepan. Bring to a boil; reduce heat, cover, keep hot.

Melt butter in large saucepan; cook onion and garlic, stirring, until onion is soft. Add rice; stir to coat in butter mixture. Stir in 1 cup of the hot stock mixture; cook, stirring, over low heat until liquid is absorbed.

Continue adding stock mixture, in 1-cup batches, stirring, until liquid is absorbed after each addition. Total cooking time should be about 35 minutes or until rice is just tender.

Add prawns, asparagus, tomato, parsley and pepper; cook, stirring, until prawns are just changed in colour and asparagus is tender.

SERVES 6
Per serving 5.6g fat; 2444kJ

Lend some flair to simple, subtly-flavoured risottos with the addition of any of these scrummy suggestions. Sprinkle them over the risotto, stir them through or serve on the side – these flavour shots will be a hit any which way.

sauteed garlic mushrooms

Heat 1 tablespoon olive oil and 40g butter in large frying pan; cook 2 cloves crushed garlic and 250g thickly sliced button mushrooms, stirring, until mushrooms are soft and browned lightly. Remove pan from heat; stir in 1 tablespoon finely chopped fresh chives.

Serves 4
Per serving
13g fat; 541kJ

crispy prosciutto

Grill 12 slices (180g) prosciutto until crisp, break in half. Top risotto with prosciutto and 1 cup (80g) parmesan cheese flakes.

Serves 8
Per serving
4.6g fat;
304kJ

crispy prosciutto

parmesan cheese flakes

sauteed garlic mushrooms

crispy garlic and herb breadcrumbs

Heat 1 tablespoon olive oil in large frying pan; cook 1¼ cups (85g) stale breadcrumbs, 1 clove crushed garlic and 1 teaspoon lemon juice over low heat, stirring, until crisp. Add ¼ cup finely chopped fresh basil leaves; cook, stirring, until breadcrumbs are browned lightly and very crisp.

Serves 6 (makes 1½ cups)
Per tablespoon 1.2g fat;
111kJ

crispy garlic and herb breadcrumbs

parsnip and carrot ribbons

Using a vegetable peeler, peel thin strips from
1 large parsnip (180g) and 1 large carrot (180g).
Heat vegetable oil in large saucepan; deep-
fry parsnip and carrot strips, separately,
in batches, until crisp and browned. Drain
on absorbent paper; serve immediately.

Serves 4

Per serving 5g fat; 161kJ

parsnip and carrot ribbons

roasted garlic tomatoes

Halve 12 medium egg tomatoes
(900g); place, cut-side up, on
wire rack in baking dish. Combine
1 teaspoon salt, 1 teaspoon
cracked black pepper, 1 teaspoon
sugar and 2 cloves crushed garlic;
sprinkle over tomato. Drizzle
2 tablespoons olive oil over
tomato; bake, uncovered, in
moderately hot oven about
30 minutes or until soft. Sprinkle
with sea salt to serve.

Serves 12

Per serving 3.1g fat; 167kJ

pesto butter

pesto butter

Beat 125g softened
butter in small bowl with
electric mixer until light
and creamy; stir in 1/4 cup
(40g) toasted pine nuts,
1/4 cup (20g) finely grated
parmesan cheese, 1/4 cup
(65g) bottled basil pesto
and 1/2 teaspoon cracked
black pepper, mix well.

Serves 6

Per tablespoon
12.9g fat; 517kJ

roasted garlic tomatoes

broad bean

risotto with crispy bacon,

parmesan and sage

1.5 litres (6 cups)
chicken stock

1/2 cup (125ml) dry
white wine

2 tablespoons olive oil

4 green onions,
chopped finely

2 cloves garlic, crushed

2 cups (400g)
arborio rice

6 bacon rashers, halved

1/2 cup (125ml) cream

1 cup (80g)
finely grated
parmesan cheese

250g frozen broad
beans, thawed, shelled

1 tablespoon coarsely
chopped fresh
sage leaves

1/2 cup (40g) parmesan
cheese flakes

Bring stock and wine to a
boil in medium saucepan;
reduce heat, cover, keep hot.
Heat oil in large saucepan;
cook onion and garlic,
stirring, until onion is soft.
Add rice, stir to coat in
oil mixture. Stir in 1 cup
of the stock mixture; cook
over low heat, stirring,
until liquid is absorbed.
Continue adding stock
mixture, in 1-cup batches,
stirring, until absorbed
after each addition. Total
cooking time should be
about 35 minutes or until
rice is just tender.
Meanwhile, cook bacon under
heated grill until browned and
crisp on both sides.
Remove pan from heat,
stir in cream, grated cheese,
beans and sage; stand,
covered, 5 minutes. Serve
topped with bacon and flaked
cheese.

SERVES 4
Per serving 39.6g fat; 3644kJ

country-style
risotto

1.5 litres (6 cups) chicken stock

1 cup (250ml) dry white wine

¾ cup (90g) frozen peas

30g butter

¼ cup (60ml) olive oil

60g pancetta, chopped finely

1 medium leek (350g), chopped finely

1 clove garlic, crushed

1 medium carrot (120g), chopped finely

1 medium parsnip (125g), chopped finely

1 trimmed celery stick (75g), chopped finely

2 cups (400g) arborio rice

2 tablespoons finely chopped fresh flat-leaf parsley

Bring stock and wine to a boil in medium saucepan; reduce heat, cover, keep hot. Boil, steam or microwave peas until just tender; drain. **Heat** butter and oil in large saucepan; cook pancetta, leek and garlic, stirring, until leek is soft. Add carrot, parsnip and celery; cook, stirring, 5 minutes. Add rice, stir to coat in oil mixture. Stir in 1 cup of the stock mixture; cook over low heat, stirring, until liquid is absorbed. **Continue** adding stock mixture, in 1-cup batches, stirring, until absorbed after each addition. Total cooking time should be about 35 minutes or until rice is just tender. Stir in peas and parsley.

SERVES 4
Per serving 24.3g fat; 2904kJ

creamy **bacon** risotto

1.5 litres (6 cups)
chicken stock

1/2 cup (125ml) dry
white wine

2 tablespoons olive oil

4 bacon rashers,
sliced thinly

500g button
mushrooms, halved

1 medium leek (350g),
sliced thinly

1 clove garlic, crushed

2 cups (400g)
arborio rice

2/3 cup (160ml) cream

1 cup (80g) finely
grated parmesan
cheese

1/2 teaspoon cracked
black pepper

1 tablespoon finely
chopped fresh
basil leaves

2 tablespoons finely
chopped fresh chives

Bring stock and wine to a boil in medium
saucepan; reduce heat, cover, keep hot.
Heat oil in large saucepan; cook bacon, stirring,
until crisp, remove from pan. Cook mushrooms
in same pan, stirring, until browned lightly. Add
leek and garlic; cook, stirring, until leek is soft.
Add rice and bacon, stir to coat in oil mixture.
Stir in 1 cup of the stock mixture; cook over
low heat, stirring, until liquid is absorbed.
Continue adding stock mixture, in 1-cup batches,
stirring, until absorbed after each addition. Total
cooking time should be about 35 minutes or until
rice is just tender. Add cream; cook, stirring,
until risotto is thick and creamy. Remove pan from
heat, stir in cheese, pepper, basil and half of the
chives. Serve topped with remaining chives.

SERVES 4
Per serving 38.9g fat; 3547kJ

roasted kumara, spinach and

1 large kumara (500g)

1.75 litres (7 cups) vegetable stock

2 tablespoons olive oil

1 small leek (200g), sliced thinly

1 clove garlic, crushed

2 cups (400g) calrose rice

200g fetta cheese, crumbled

100g baby spinach leaves

basil pesto

1 cup firmly packed fresh basil leaves

1 clove garlic, crushed

1/4 cup (60ml) olive oil

1/4 cup (60ml) buttermilk

2 tablespoons coarsely grated parmesan cheese

Cut kumara into 3cm pieces. Place kumara in oiled non-stick baking dish; roast, uncovered, in hot oven about 20 minutes or until browned and just tender, turning once during cooking.

Meanwhile, bring stock to a boil in medium saucepan; reduce heat, cover, keep hot.

Heat oil in large saucepan; cook leek and garlic, stirring, until leek is soft. Add rice, stir to coat in oil mixture. Stir in 1 cup of the stock; cook over low heat, stirring, until liquid is absorbed.

Continue adding stock, in 1-cup batches, stirring, until absorbed after each addition. Total cooking time should be about 35 minutes or until rice is just tender.

Remove pan from heat, gently stir in kumara, fetta and spinach. Serve topped with Basil Pesto.

Basil Pesto Blend or process ingredients until smooth. Cover surface with plastic wrap until ready to use.

SERVES 4
Per serving 39.6g fat; 3668kJ

fetta risotto with basil pesto

tuna and
mushroom risotto

2 medium
carrots (240g)

2 tablespoons olive oil

1 medium leek (350g),
sliced thinly

400g button
mushrooms,
sliced thinly

2 cups (400g)
calrose rice

1 litre (4 cups)
chicken stock

1 cup (125g) frozen
peas, thawed

425g can
tuna, drained

Cut carrots into thin strips. Heat oil in large
saucepan; cook leek, mushroom and carrot,
stirring, until leek is soft. Add rice, stir to coat in
oil mixture. Add stock; bring to a boil. Reduce
heat; simmer, covered, 15 minutes, stirring
midway through cooking. Stir in peas and tuna,
remove from heat; stand, covered, 10 minutes.

SERVES 4
Per serving 13.3g fat; 2633kJ

quick and easy chicken and
vegetable risotto

2 tablespoons olive oil

1 medium brown onion (150g), chopped finely

2 cups (400g) calrose rice

3 cups (750ml) chicken stock

500g frozen mixed vegetables

2 cups (340g) coarsely shredded cooked chicken

1/2 cup (125ml) cream

1 cup (120g) coarsely grated smoked cheddar cheese

1/2 cup (40g) finely grated parmesan cheese

Heat oil in large saucepan; cook onion, stirring, until soft. Add rice, stir to coat in oil mixture. Add stock and vegetables; bring to a boil. Reduce heat; simmer, covered, 15 minutes, stirring midway through cooking. Stir in remaining ingredients, remove from heat; stand, covered, 10 minutes.

SERVES 4
Per serving 41.7g fat; 3862kJ

vodka mussels
with lemon dill risotto

1 litre (4 cups)
vegetable stock

24 medium (600g)
black mussels

2 tablespoons olive oil

2 small brown onions (160g),
chopped finely

1½ cups (300g) arborio rice

2 cloves garlic, crushed

2 red thai chillies,
chopped finely

⅓ cup coarsely chopped
fresh parsley stems

⅓ cup (80ml) vodka

2 tablespoons finely
grated lemon rind

2 tablespoons finely
chopped fresh dill

Bring stock to a boil in medium saucepan; reduce heat, cover, keep hot. Scrub mussels, remove beards. **Heat** half of the oil in large saucepan; cook half of the onion, stirring, until soft. Add rice, stir to coat in oil mixture. Stir in 1 cup of the stock; cook over low heat, stirring, until liquid is absorbed. **Continue** adding stock, in 1-cup batches, stirring, until absorbed after each addition. Total cooking time should be about 35 minutes or until rice is just tender.

Meanwhile, heat remaining oil in medium frying pan; cook remaining onion, garlic and chilli, stirring, until onion is soft. Stir in parsley and vodka; cook, stirring, 2 minutes. Stir in mussels; cook, covered, about 10 minutes or until mussels open. Discard any that do not open. **Drain** mussels over medium heatproof bowl; reserve liquid. Pick out mussels, shake off cooking solids, place mussels in medium bowl. Stir reserved liquid into risotto; cook risotto, stirring, until liquid is absorbed. Stir rind and dill into risotto; serve with mussels.

SERVES 4
Per serving 11.1g fat; 1900kJ

mushroom
capsicum risotto

1 tablespoon olive oil

1 medium brown onion
(150g), chopped finely

2 cloves garlic,
crushed

1¹/₂ cups (300g)
short-grain rice

3¹/₂ cups (875ml)
vegetable stock

2 teaspoons olive
oil, extra

125g button
mushrooms,
sliced thinly

2 medium zucchini
(240g), sliced thinly

1 medium green
capsicum (200g),
chopped finely

1 medium red
capsicum (200g),
chopped finely

2 small tomatoes
(260g), chopped finely

¹/₄ cup (30g) seeded
black olives

¹/₂ cup (40g) parmesan
cheese flakes

Heat oil in large saucepan; cook onion and
garlic, stirring, until onion is soft. Add rice, stir
to coat in oil mixture. Add stock; bring to a boil.
Reduce heat; simmer, covered, 15 minutes,
stirring midway through cooking. Remove pan
from heat; stand, covered, 10 minutes.
Meanwhile, heat extra oil in large frying pan;
cook mushrooms, zucchini, capsicums and
tomato, stirring, until vegetables are tender.
Stir vegetables and olives into risotto; serve
topped with flaked cheese.

SERVES 4
Per serving 11.9g fat; 1902kJ

pork, pine nut and
cointreau risotto

500g pork fillets

1 tablespoon
teriyaki marinade

1 teaspoon finely
grated orange rind

3 cloves garlic,
crushed

1 large brown onion
(200g), chopped finely

2 cups (400g)
arborio rice

1.25 litres (5 cups)
chicken stock

½ cup (125ml) dry
white wine

2 tablespoons
Cointreau

150g baby
spinach leaves

2 tablespoons pine
nuts, toasted

2 tablespoons coarsely
chopped fresh lemon
thyme

Place pork on rack in baking dish; brush
with combined marinade and rind. Bake,
uncovered, in hot oven 20 minutes. Cover
pork, stand 5 minutes; slice thinly.

Meanwhile, cook garlic and onion in heated,
oiled large saucepan, stirring, until onion is soft.

Add rice, stock, wine and Cointreau; bring
to a boil. Reduce heat; simmer, covered,
15 minutes, stirring midway through cooking.
Remove from heat; stand, covered, 10 minutes.
Stir in spinach, pine nuts, thyme and pork.

SERVES 4
Per serving 9.8g fat; 2738kJ

thai-flavoured

200g green beans, chopped coarsely

1 tablespoon peanut oil

500g chicken tenderloins

1 medium brown onion (150g), chopped finely

1 tablespoon red massaman curry paste

2 cups (400g) arborio rice

2¹/₂ cups (625ml) chicken stock

1²/₃ cups (400ml) coconut milk

2 tablespoons finely chopped fresh coriander leaves

¹/₂ cup (75g) roasted unsalted peanuts

2 tablespoons fresh coriander leaves

hicken risotto

Boil, steam or microwave beans until just tender, rinse under cold water; drain.
Heat oil in large saucepan; cook chicken, stirring, until browned all over and cooked through, remove from pan.
Cook onion and paste in same pan, stirring, until fragrant. Add rice, stir to coat in oil mixture. Add stock and coconut milk; bring to a boil. Reduce heat; simmer, covered, 15 minutes, stirring midway through cooking. Remove pan from heat; stand, covered, 10 minutes.
Stir in beans, chicken and chopped coriander; serve topped with peanuts and coriander leaves.

SERVES 4
Per serving 45.2g fat; 3943kJ

char-grilled lamb
risotto with tomato salsa

500g lamb fillets

1/4 cup (65g) bottled basil pesto

1.5 litres (6 cups) chicken stock

3/4 cup (180ml) dry white wine

2 tablespoons tomato paste

2 tablespoons olive oil

1 medium brown onion (150g), sliced thinly

2 cloves garlic, crushed

2 cups (400g) arborio rice

tomato salsa

2 medium tomatoes (380g), seeded, chopped finely

100g firm fetta cheese, chopped finely

1/2 cup (60g) seeded black olives, chopped finely

2 tablespoons olive oil

1 tablespoon finely chopped fresh mint leaves

Combine lamb and pesto in medium bowl; cover, stand 10 minutes.

Bring stock, wine and tomato paste to a boil in medium saucepan; reduce heat, cover, keep hot.

Heat oil in large saucepan; cook onion and garlic, stirring, until onion is soft. Add rice, stir to coat in oil mixture. Stir in 1 cup of the stock mixture; cook over low heat, stirring, until liquid is absorbed.

Continue adding stock mixture, in 1-cup batches, stirring, until absorbed after each addition. Total cooking time should be about 35 minutes or until rice is just tender.

Meanwhile, cook lamb on heated oiled grill plate (or grill or barbecue) until browned all over and cooked as desired; slice thickly.

Remove risotto from heat, stir in lamb; serve topped with Tomato Salsa.

Tomato Salsa Combine ingredients in medium bowl.

SERVES 4
Per serving 35.4g fat; 3714kJ

baked risotto with salami
and char-grilled capsicum

100g sliced
mild salami,
chopped coarsely

2 cups (400g)
ricotta cheese

1 cup (200g)
char-grilled capsicum
in oil, drained

1 cup (70g) stale
breadcrumbs

1/2 cup (40g)
finely grated parmesan
cheese

40g butter, melted

risotto

20g butter

1 medium brown onion
(150g), chopped finely

1 cup (200g)
calrose rice

3 cups (750ml)
chicken stock

1/2 cup (60g) coarsely
grated smoked
cheddar cheese

1/2 cup (125ml) cream

Spoon half of the hot Risotto over base of
shallow 2-litre (8-cup) oiled ovenproof dish.
Top with salami and half of the ricotta. Spoon
over remaining Risotto; top with remaining
ricotta and capsicum. Sprinkle with combined
remaining ingredients.

Bake, uncovered, in very hot oven about
15 minutes or until browned and heated through.

Risotto Heat butter in medium saucepan; cook
onion, stirring, until soft. Add rice, stir to coat in
butter mixture. Add stock; bring to a boil. Reduce
heat; simmer, covered, 15 minutes, stirring midway
through cooking. Remove from heat; stand,
covered, 10 minutes. Stir in cheese and cream.

SERVES 4
Per serving 64g fat; 4105kJ

mushroom, spinach
and lemon risotto

2 medium brown
onions (300g),
chopped finely

3 cloves garlic,
crushed

1 tablespoon finely
grated lemon rind

300g button
mushrooms, halved

2 cups (400g)
arborio rice

1.5 litres (6 cups)
chicken stock

1 cup (250ml) dry
white wine

300g baby
spinach leaves

2 tablespoons coarsely
chopped fresh lemon
thyme

Heat oiled large saucepan; cook onion, garlic, rind and mushrooms, stirring, until mushrooms are browned. Add rice, stock and wine; bring to a boil. Reduce heat; simmer, covered, 15 minutes, stirring midway through cooking. **Remove** pan from heat; stand, covered, 10 minutes. Gently stir in spinach and lemon thyme.

SERVES 4
Per serving 2.6g fat; 2049kJ

cheesy pine nut

and char-grilled

vegetable risotto

1.25 litres (5 cups) chicken stock

1 cup (250ml) dry white wine

1 cup (250ml) milk

270g jar char-grilled vegetables in oil

1 medium brown onion (150g), chopped finely

1 clove garlic, crushed

2 cups (400g) arborio rice

1/4 cup (60ml) cream

1 cup (80g) finely grated parmesan cheese

1 tablespoon finely chopped fresh basil leaves

1/2 cup (80g) pine nuts, toasted

1/2 cup (40g) parmesan cheese flakes

freshly ground black pepper

Bring stock and wine to a boil in medium saucepan, add milk; reduce heat, cover, keep hot. Drain vegetables over small bowl; reserve vegetables and 2 tablespoons of the oil.

Heat reserved oil in large saucepan; cook onion and garlic, stirring, until onion is soft. Add rice, stir to coat in oil mixture. Stir in 1 cup of stock mixture; cook over low heat, stirring, until liquid is absorbed.

Continue adding stock mixture, in 1-cup batches, stirring, until absorbed after each addition. Total cooking time should be about 35 minutes or until rice is just tender. Remove pan from heat, stir in coarsely chopped reserved vegetables, cream, grated cheese, basil and half of the pine nuts.

Serve topped with remaining pine nuts, flaked cheese and pepper.

SERVES 4
Per serving 45.7g fat; 4109kJ

54 meatball risotto

with oregano and tomatoes

40g butter

1 medium brown onion
(150g), sliced thinly

2 cloves garlic, crushed

1 tablespoon finely
chopped fresh
oregano leaves

2 cups (400g) arborio rice

1/2 cup (125ml) dry
red wine

1 cup (250ml) bottled
tomato pasta sauce

1 litre (4 cups)
chicken stock

1/4 cup (60ml) cream

1 cup (80g) parmesan
cheese flakes

meatballs

500g minced beef

1 clove garlic, crushed

1 cup (70g) stale
breadcrumbs

1 egg yolk

2 teaspoons finely chopped
fresh
oregano leaves

Heat butter in large saucepan; cook onion, garlic and oregano, stirring, until onion is soft. Add rice, stir to coat in butter mixture.
Add wine; cook over low heat, stirring, until liquid is absorbed. Add pasta sauce and stock, bring to a boil; reduce heat, simmer, covered, 10 minutes.
Remove lid; simmer, stirring, about 15 minutes or until liquid is absorbed and rice is just tender. Remove pan from heat, stir in Meatballs and cream; stand, covered, 5 minutes. Serve topped with flaked cheese.
Meatballs Combine ingredients in medium bowl. Shape level tablespoons of mixture into balls; cook in heated oiled large non-stick frying pan, shaking pan occasionally, until meatballs are browned all over and cooked through, drain on absorbent paper.

SERVES 4
Per serving 34.3g fat; 3852kJ

chicken and
lemon risotto

60g butter

1 large brown onion
(200g), chopped finely

2 cloves garlic,
crushed

1½ cups (300g)
arborio rice

1 litre (4 cups)
chicken stock

½ cup (125ml) dry
white wine

2 cups (340g) chopped
cooked chicken

2 teaspoons finely
grated lemon rind

4 green onions,
chopped finely

2 tablespoons finely
chopped fresh
flat-leaf parsley

¼ cup (20g)
finely grated parmesan
cheese

Heat butter in large saucepan; cook onion and garlic, stirring, until onion is soft. Add rice, stir to coat in butter mixture. Add stock and wine; bring to a boil. Reduce heat; simmer, uncovered, stirring occasionally, about 15 minutes or until rice is tender and most of the liquid is absorbed. **Add** remaining ingredients; cook, stirring, until hot.

SERVES 4
Per serving 21.4g fat; 2514kJ

spicy chicken and
csabai risotto

1.375 litres (5½ cups)
chicken stock

2 tablespoons olive oil

125g piece csabai sausage,
sliced thinly

5 (550g) chicken thigh
fillets, quartered

1 large brown onion (200g),
chopped finely

1 clove garlic, crushed

1 teaspoon dried
crushed chillies

2 cups (400g) arborio rice

½ cup (125ml) dry white wine

400g can tomatoes

2 tablespoons coarsely
chopped fresh flat-leaf parsley

Bring stock to a boil in medium saucepan; reduce heat, cover, keep hot.
Heat oil in large saucepan; cook sausage, stirring, until browned and
crisp, drain on absorbent paper. Cook chicken in same pan, stirring, until
browned all over. Add onion, garlic and chilli; cook, stirring, until onion is
soft. Add rice, stir to coat in oil mixture. Add wine and undrained crushed
tomatoes; cook over low heat, stirring, until liquid is absorbed. Stir in
1 cup of the stock; cook over low heat, stirring, until liquid is absorbed.
Continue adding stock in 1-cup batches, stirring, until absorbed after
each addition. Total cooking time should be about 35 minutes or until
rice is just tender. Remove pan from heat, stir in sausage; serve
sprinkled with parsley.

SERVES 4
Per serving 30.6g fat; 3491kJ

herb risotto with

creamy veal and mushrooms

1/4 cup (60ml) olive oil

1 medium leek (350g), sliced thinly

2 cups (400g) arborio rice

1 litre (4 cups) chicken stock

2 tablespoons olive oil, extra

4 (500g) veal schnitzels, halved

250g button mushrooms, sliced thickly

2 cloves garlic, crushed

1/2 cup (125ml) dry white wine

300ml cream

1 teaspoon seeded mustard

1/2 cup (40g) finely grated parmesan cheese

1 tablespoon finely chopped fresh oregano leaves

2 tablespoons finely chopped fresh basil leaves

2 tablespoons finely chopped fresh flat-leaf parsley

Heat oil in large saucepan; cook leek, stirring, until soft. Add rice, stir to coat in oil mixture. Stir in stock; bring to a boil. Reduce heat; simmer, covered, 15 minutes, stirring midway through cooking. Remove pan from heat; stand, covered, 10 minutes.

Meanwhile, heat extra oil in large non-stick frying pan; cook veal until browned both sides, remove from pan. Cook mushrooms and garlic in same pan, stirring, until mushrooms are browned lightly. Add wine, bring to a boil. Add cream and mustard; simmer, uncovered, until thickened.

Return veal to pan; simmer, uncovered, until veal is heated through. Just before serving, stir cheese and herbs into risotto; serve topped with veal mixture.

SERVES 4
Per serving 63.7g fat; 4664kJ

glossary

bacon rashers also known as slices of bacon; made from pork side, cured and smoked.

breadcrumbs, stale one- or two-day-old bread made into crumbs by grating, blending or processing.

broad beans also known as fava beans; available fresh, frozen or canned. Best when peeled twice (discard the long pod and the tough, pale-green inner shell).

butter use salted or unsalted ("sweet") butter; 125g is equal to 1 stick butter.

buttermilk despite the implication of its name, is low in fat. Commercially made, by a method similar to yogurt.

capsicum also known as bell pepper or, simply, pepper. Discard membranes and seeds before use.

cheese

fetta: crumbly-textured sheep- or goat-milk cheese.

parmesan: sharp-tasting, dry, hard cheese made from skim or part-skim milk and aged at least a year.

ricotta: sweet, moist, fresh curd cheese having low fat content.

chicken, tenderloin thin strip of meat under breast.

coconut milk unsweetened coconut milk available in cans.

cointreau citrus-flavoured liqueur.

cream also known as pure cream and pouring cream; has no additives and a minimum 35% fat content.

csabai sausage Hungarian in origin, a dried pork or beef sausage flavoured with pimiento, paprika and black peppercorns.

eggplant also known as aubergine.

fennel also known as finocchio or anise; eaten raw in salads or braised or fried as a vegetable accompaniment.

garam masala a blend of spices, originating in North India; based on varying proportions of cardamom, cinnamon, clove, coriander, fennel and cumin, roasted and ground together.

herbs if fresh are not specified, we used dried (not ground) herbs in the ratio of 1:4 for fresh herbs.

kumara Polynesian name of orange-fleshed sweet potato, often confused with yam.

mushrooms

button: small, cultivated white mushrooms having a delicate, subtle flavour.

flat: often misnamed as field mushrooms; large, soft, flat mushrooms with a rich, earthy flavour.

porcini, dried: earthy tasting dried mushroom; place in hot water to reconstitute before use.

mustard, seeded also known as wholegrain. A French-style coarse-grain mustard made from crushed mustard seeds and Dijon-style French mustard.

oil

olive: made from the pressing of tree-ripened olives. "Extra light" or "light" describes the flavour, not the fat levels. "Extra virgin" and "virgin" are best quality olive oils, obtained from the first pressings of the olives.

vegetable: any of a number of oils sourced from plants rather than animal fats.

onion, green also known as scallion or (incorrectly) shallot; onion picked before bulb has formed. Has long, bright-green edible stalk.

pancetta an Italian salt-cured pork roll, usually cut from the belly; bacon can be substituted, if unavailable.

peperoni sausage made of minced pork and beef with added fat; flavoured with hot red pepper.

pork fillet skinless, boneless eye-fillet cut from the loin.

prawns also known as shrimp.

prosciutto salted-cured, air-dried (unsmoked), pressed ham; usually sold in paper-thin slices, ready to eat.

pumpkin also known as squash; we prefer to use butternut pumpkin.

rice
arborio: small, round-grained white rice that absorbs a large amount of liquid.
calrose: medium-grain; can be used instead of both long- and short-grain varieties.
short-grain: fat, almost round grain having high starch content.

saffron stigma of a member of the crocus family, available in strands or ground form; imparts yellow-orange colour to food once infused. The best saffron is the most expensive spice in the world.

seafood marinara mix a mixture of uncooked, chopped seafood.

spinach also known as English spinach and, incorrectly, silverbeet. Tender green leaves are good raw in salads or added to soups, stir-fries and stews just before serving.

stock 1 cup (250ml) stock is the equivalent of 1 cup (250ml) water plus one crumbled stock cube or 1 teaspoon stock powder.

sugar, brown soft, finely granulated sugar retaining molasses for its characteristic colour and flavour.

teriyaki marinade a blend of soy sauce, wine, vinegar and spices.

tomato
cherry: tiny, perfectly round tomatoes with sweet flavour.
egg: also called plum or Roma tomatoes; small, oval-shaped.
paste: thick, triple-concentrated paste made from tomato puree; used for flavouring stews, soups, sauces, casseroles, etc.

vinegar, balsamic authentic only from the province of Modena, Italy; made from a regional wine of white Trebbiano grapes, processed then aged in antique wooden casks.

zucchini also known as courgette.

index

These conversions are approximate only, but the difference between an exact and the approximate conversion of various liquid and dry measures is minimal and will not affect your cooking results.

Measuring equipment

The difference between one country's measuring cups and another's is, at most, within a 2 or 3 teaspoon variance. (For the record, 1 Australian metric measuring cup holds approximately 250ml.) The most accurate way of measuring dry ingredients is to weigh them. For liquids, use a clear glass or plastic jug having metric markings.

Note: NZ, Canada, USA and UK all use 15ml tablespoons. Australian tablespoons measure 20ml.
All cup and spoon measurements are level.

How to measure

When using graduated measuring cups, shake dry ingredients loosely into the appropriate cup. Do not tap the cup on a bench or tightly pack the ingredients unless directed to do so. Level the top of measuring cups and measuring spoons with a knife. When measuring liquids, place a clear glass or plastic jug having metric markings on a flat surface to check accuracy at eye level.

Dry Measures

metric	imperial
15g	½ oz
30g	1oz
60g	2oz
90g	3oz
125g	4oz (¼lb)
155g	5oz
185g	6oz
220g	7oz
250g	8oz (½lb)
280g	9oz
315g	10oz
345g	11oz
375g	12oz (¾lb)
410g	13oz
440g	14oz
470g	15oz
500g	16oz (1lb)
750g	24oz (1½lb)
1kg	32oz (2lb)

We use large eggs having an average weight of 60g.

Liquid Measures

metric	imperial
30ml	1 fluid oz
60ml	2 fluid oz
100ml	3 fluid oz
125ml	4 fluid oz
150ml	5 fluid oz (¼pint/1 gill)
190ml	6 fluid oz
250ml (1cup)	8 fluid oz
300ml	10 fluid oz (½pint)
500ml	16 fluid oz
600ml	20 fluid oz (1 pint)
1000ml (1litre)	1¾ pints

Helpful Measures

metric	imperial
3mm	⅛ in
6mm	¼ in
1cm	½ in
2cm	¾ in
2.5cm	1in
6cm	2½in
8cm	3in
20cm	8in
23cm	9in
25cm	10in
30cm	12in (1ft)

Oven Temperatures

These oven temperatures are only a guide.
Always check the manufacturer's manual.

	°C (Celsius)	°F (Fahrenheit)	Gas Mark
Very slow	120	250	1
Slow	150	300	2
Moderately slow	160	325	3
Moderate	180 –190	350 – 375	4
Moderately hot	200 – 210	400 – 425	5
Hot	220 – 230	450 – 475	6
Very hot	240 – 250	500 – 525	7

at your fingertips

These elegant slipcovers store up to 10 mini books and make the books instantly accessible.

And the metric measuring cups and spoons make following our recipes a piece of cake.

Book Holder
Australia and overseas:
$8.95 (incl. GST).

Metric Measuring Set
Australia: $6.50 (incl. GST).
New Zealand: $A8.00.
Elsewhere: $A9.95.
Prices include postage and handling. This offer is available in all countries.

Photocopy and complete coupon below

Mail or fax Photocopy and complete the coupon below and post to ACP Books Reader Offer, ACP Publishing, GPO Box 4967, Sydney NSW 2001, *or* fax to (02) 9267 4967.

Phone Have your credit card details ready, then phone 136 116 (Mon-Fri, 8.00am-6.00pm; Sat, 8.00am-6.00pm).

Australian residents We accept the credit cards listed on the coupon, money orders and cheques.
Overseas residents We accept the credit cards listed on the coupon, drafts in $A drawn on an Australian bank, and also UK, NZ and US cheques in the currency of the country of issue. Credit card charges are at the exchange rate current at the time of payment.

- -

❑ **Book Holder**   ❑ **Metric Measuring Set**
Please indicate number(s) required.

Mr/Mrs/Ms _____

Address _____

_____

Postcode _____ Country _____

Ph: Business hours ( ) _____

I enclose my cheque/money order for $ _____ payable to ACP Publishing.

OR: please charge $ _____ to my ❑ Bankcard ❑ Mastercard

❑ Visa ❑ American Express ❑ Diners Club

Expiry date ____ /____

| | | | | | | | | | | | | | | | | | |
Card number

Cardholder's signature _____

Please allow up to 30 days delivery within Australia.
Allow up to 6 weeks for overseas deliveries.
Both offers expire 31/12/05. HLMR04

Food director Pamela Clark
Food editor Karen Hammial
Assistant food editor Kathy McGarry
Assistant recipe editor Elizabeth Hooper
ACP BOOKS
Editorial director Susan Tomnay
Creative director Hieu Chi Nguyen
Senior editor Julie Collard
Designer Caryl Wiggins
Publishing manager (sales) Brian Cearnes
Sales & marketing coordinator Caroline Lowry
Publishing manager (rights & new projects) Jane Hazell
Pre-press by Harry Palmer
Production manager Carol Currie
Business manager Seymour Cohen
Business analyst Martin Howes
Chief executive officer John Alexander
Group publisher Pat Ingram
Publisher Sue Wannan
Editor-in-chief Deborah Thomas
Produced by ACP Books, Sydney.
Printing by Dai Nippon Printing in Korea.
Published by ACP Publishing Pty Limited, 54 Park St, Sydney;
GPO Box 4088, Sydney, NSW 2001.
Ph: (02) 9282 8618 Fax: (02) 9267 9438.
www.acpbooks.com.au
To order books phone 136 116.
Send recipe enquiries to
Recipeenquiries@acp.com.au
Australia Distributed by Network Services, GPO Box 4088, Sydney, NSW 2001.
Ph: (02) 9282 8777 Fax: (02) 9264 3278.
United Kingdom Distributed by Australian Consolidated Press (UK), Moulton Park Business Centre, Red House Road, Moulton Park, Northampton, NN3 6AQ. Ph: (01604) 497 531 Fax: (01604) 497 533 acpukltd@aol.com
Canada Distributed by Whitecap Books Ltd, 351 Lynn Ave, North Vancouver, BC, V7J 2C4, Ph: (604) 980 9852 Fax: (604) 980 8197 customerservice@whitecap.ca
www.whitecap.ca
New Zealand Distributed by Netlink Distribution Company, ACP Media Centre, Cnr Fanshawe and Beaumont Streets, Westhaven, Auckland; PO Box 47906, Ponsonby, Auckland, NZ.
Ph: (09) 366 9966 ask@ndcnz.co.nz
South Africa Distributed by PSD Promotions, 30 Diesel Road, Isando, Gauteng, Johannesburg; PO Box 1175, Isando, 1600, Gauteng, Johannesburg. Ph: (27 11) 392 6065/7 Fax: (27 11) 392 6079/80 orders@psdprom.co.za

Make it tonight: Risotto

Includes index.
ISBN 1 86396 229 8

1. Cookery (rice). 2. Risotto.
I. Title: Australian Women's Weekly.
(Series: Australian Women's Weekly make it tonight mini series).
641.6318

© ACP Publishing Pty Limited 2001
ABN 18 053 273 546

Cover Marinated lamb, rosemary and garlic risotto, page 16.
Stylist Vicki Liley
Photographer Mark O'Meara
Back cover at left, Roasted risotto-filled capsicums, page 15; at right, Thai-flavoured chicken risotto, page 46.
First published 2001. Reprinted 2004.